Who Is Dwayne "The Rock" Johnson?

Who Is Dwayne "The Rock" Johnson?

by James Buckley Jr.

illustrated by Gregory Copeland

Penguin Workshop

For Gordo—JB

To my beautiful mother, with love—GC

PENGUIN WORKSHOP
An Imprint of Penguin Random House LLC, New York

Visit us online at www.penguinrandomhouse.com.

Library of Congress Cataloging-in-Publication Data is available upon request.

ISBN 9780593226377 (paperback)   10 9 8 7 6 5 4 3 2 1
ISBN 9780593226384 (library binding)   10 9 8 7 6 5 4 3 2 1

Contents

Who Is Dwayne "The Rock" Johnson?

Dwayne Johnson stands on the arm of a huge crane, hundreds of feet above a busy city street. In front of him, a skyscraper is on fire. He needs to get inside that burning building. His family is in there, held captive by armed villains.

Behind him, a group of men race to stop him. There is only one thing to do.

Jump!

Bullets ping everywhere around him as Dwayne sprints toward the end of the crane. When he reaches it, he leaps, arms windmilling, legs churning in midair. He plummets toward his goal, an open window in the side of the building.

His powerful, muscular body smashes into

the glass wall as his mighty hands grip the window ledge. Can he hold on?

He can! Dwayne climbs over broken glass to reach the inside of the building!

The director yells, "Cut!"

The scene in the movie *Skyscraper* was over. Dwayne stood up with a huge grin on his face. He had just filmed another amazing action-movie moment, one of dozens that have made him the biggest movie star on the planet. In more than twenty hugely popular films, Dwayne has used his oversize muscles—and a personality that is even bigger—to thrill and entertain fans.

A former pro wrestling star known as "The Rock," Dwayne worked hard to become an actor. His inspiring story and constantly positive attitude have made him an international hero. More than 200 million people follow his Instagram feed, where he shares details of his life, and some of his wisdom, with the world. Dwayne believes "the road to success and greatness is always paved with hard work. Chase your greatness!"

CHAPTER 1
Just Plain Dwayne

Dwayne Johnson was born in Hayward, California, on May 2, 1972. When Dwayne was a baby, he and his family moved often. By the time Dwayne was in kindergarten, he had lived in five different states! The family moved often because Dwayne's father, Rocky, was a professional wrestler, and took his family with him as he traveled from event to event.

Rocky had met his wife, Ata, when he wrestled with her father, Peter Maivia, who was also a professional wrestler. Ata's full name was Feagaimaleata Fitisemanu Maivia. Her family came from the Pacific islands of Samoa and Hawaii. Peter had won championships in Hawaii and in the World Wrestling Federation (WWF),

Dwayne and his father, Rocky Johnson

the biggest organization in the sport. The WWF put on events all over the United States, attracting huge audiences. WWF wrestlers were big personalities, great showmen and women, and powerful athletes. They were also entertainers.

When Dwayne was about nine, the family lived in Hawaii, where Rocky wrestled and Ata was able to spend time with her father and her large Samoan family. Dwayne learned a lot about his heritage on the island. He saw his grandfather's large Samoan tattoos. He also watched the respect that Peter Maivia had in the wrestling community. Peter died of cancer in 1982, and Dwayne was among thousands who attended his grandfather's funeral.

Rocky's career kept the family moving from place to place. Before he reached high school, the Johnson family had lived in fourteen states. It was difficult for Dwayne to change schools so often, as he was always having to find new friends. Fitting into a new place over and over was difficult. Dwayne was friendly and outgoing, but he was also very big, which made him stand out even more. He was well over six feet tall in junior high, and was very strong like Rocky. In many of his new schools, other big students wanted to challenge him. "I was always the new kid, so that made me a target," he says.

During a period when the family was back in Hawaii, Dwayne got in real trouble. He and some other teenagers were caught stealing. He was arrested several times. "It was when I was in the ninth grade. I was doing stupid stuff and the cops came into the class [to arrest me]. I was humiliated more than anything."

Dwayne and his parents left Hawaii again not long after, and settled in Bethlehem, Pennsylvania, for Dwayne's second year in high school. Not long after he arrived, Dwayne was caught by a teacher named Jody Cwik using the bathroom in the teacher's lounge. Dwayne later said, "That was the day that changed everything." Mr. Cwik was the school's football coach. After Dwayne apologized the next day, Mr. Cwik asked him to join the football team.

CHAPTER 2
Hurricane Dwayne

With Mr. Cwik and others as his coaches, Dwayne soon became a high school football star. He was six feet four inches tall and weighed 230 pounds. He had very broad shoulders, and he was extremely fast for a person of his size. As a junior, he played tight end and defensive end. Thanks to his outgoing personality, Dwayne was also named a team captain.

In his senior year, he was named an all-American while making fourteen sacks and more than one hundred tackles. Dwayne thought that the University of Miami would be a good place for him to play. The Miami Hurricanes were one of the top teams in the country. They also played with a lot of personality and attitude,

Dwayne and Coach Cwik

which Dwayne liked. So he contacted Miami's coaches by calling them himself, which was a very unusual move. Most schools scouted players, but Dwayne chose the university he was interested in and contacted them. The coaches were impressed by Dwayne's confidence and by his skill. In February 1989, he signed up to play football for the Hurricanes.

College was a big change for Dwayne. He was surrounded by athletes who had been the best in their own towns. Suddenly, even though he had grown to six feet five inches and 235 pounds, he was not the biggest guy on the field anymore. Many teammates were bigger than Dwayne, and they all were as confident as he was. He had to work harder than ever, practicing twice a day in the summer before the 1989 season, and lifting weights every day. Unfortunately, ten days before the first game, he suffered a bad shoulder injury while making a tackle in practice.

He had shoulder surgery and missed the entire season.

For an active person like Dwayne, it was a difficult time. He was away from home and could only get support from his parents by phone. He sulked at missing football and didn't attend classes. In December, the football team put him on probation because he was failing. "Humiliating? Absolutely," Dwayne remembered. "I had let my parents down, I had let my teammates and coaches down, and I had let myself down."

While he was recovering from his injury and improving his grades, Dwayne met Dany Garcia. She was a student at Miami studying business. Dany introduced herself to Dwayne at a nightclub. Dwayne and Dany started dating, but her parents were not happy. They were from Cuba and they did not approve of Dwayne because his father was Black. It would be a long time before they accepted Dwayne.

Dwayne and Dany at the University of Miami

The next year, Dwayne's grades improved, and he was back on the football team by the start of the 1991 season. The Hurricanes went undefeated. With Dwayne at defensive end, the Hurricanes beat Nebraska, 22–0, in the Orange Bowl and were named the top-ranked college team in the nation, along with the Washington Huskies.

Dwayne played two more seasons at Miami. As a senior, he suffered a painful back injury, but he kept playing. After he graduated, he was disappointed that no team from the National Football League (NFL) signed him. So Dwayne went to play in the Canadian Football League (CFL) for the Calgary Stampeders. Instead of making millions in the NFL as he had hoped, he was paid $250 a week. But Dwayne's time in Canada was short. Though he had practiced with the team for two months, the Stampeders cut him from the team before he had even played in a game!

Dwayne was at a low point. His dream of a pro football career was over. He had just seven dollars in his wallet, and Dany's parents still did not accept him. It was time for a new dream, so he looked to the family business. Dwayne asked Rocky to train him to become a pro wrestler.

CHAPTER 3
The Birth of The Rock

Dwayne moved to Tampa, Florida, to be near his father and to begin training for a career as a wrestler. Dany stayed in Miami, where she had found a job.

To support himself as he learned to wrestle, Dwayne worked as a personal trainer. He found that he was very good at inspiring people to work hard and get in shape. He used his own story as an example, talking about how he had bounced back from injuries and disappointment. Soon he was one of the most popular trainers at the gym.

When his work day was over, he headed to the wrestling ring, where Rocky showed him all the right moves. Wrestlers in the WWF need to be able to do all their moves safely, but also with style and flair. Rocky showed Dwayne headlocks and lifts. He taught him how to "lock up," or start a match, and how to fall correctly when thrown. They practiced dropkicks, in which one wrestler leaps to kick the other in the chest, often with both feet. Rocky taught Dwayne how to "spot," or plan a series of moves with another wrestler.

Early in his training, Dwayne felt that he was on the right path. "I knew in my heart I had found my calling. I could not have been more certain," he later said. He called Dany to let her know how happy he was.

To move from practice to the real thing, Dwayne repeated what he had done to find his college football home—he got on the phone. He called Pat Patterson, a wrestling trainer for the WWF. Pat had been a tag-team partner with Rocky and had met Dwayne years earlier.

Pat remembered Rocky's son and agreed to watch him work out. Dany came up to Tampa for the workout, along with Dwayne's mom, Ata.

Rocky and Dwayne performed in the ring for Pat. At one point, Dwayne fell to the mat, holding his back and screaming in pain. Dany shouted for the men to stop. Dwayne got up easily. He had to explain to her that he was just acting. In wrestling language, he was "selling." Not only was Dwayne a great athlete, he was becoming a great showman, too.

The physical action of professional wrestling is very real, with highly trained athletes jumping, lifting, grabbing, and throwing each other. People can and do get injured sometimes. But the punches don't always hurt as much as they seem to.

The WWF recognized Dwayne's talent and signed him to a contract in 1996. If he made it to the top level of the sport, he could be paid $150,000. It was a huge increase from his pro football earnings. Dwayne still had to work hard to earn that much. He started wrestling in a lower-level group called the United States Wrestling Association. It was based in Memphis, Tennessee. Once again, Dwayne was on the road. He performed all over the South with the USWA for several months, wrestling in school gyms, barns, and recreation centers in front of cheering crowds.

With the USWA, Dwayne created his first wrestling character, Flex Kavana, a name he made up. After six months with the USWA, Dwayne wrestled in his first WWF event on November 16, 1996. On that day, he became the first wrestler to ever follow his father and grandfather to the WWF.

The company's owner, Vince McMahon, decided Dwayne's character would be called

Rocky Maivia to honor Dwayne's family legacy. Using that name, Dwayne performed at New York City's Madison Square Garden, one of the most famous sports arenas in the world. He won

his first match, and as 22,000 people chanted his new name, "that moment changed my life," Dwayne remembered. This marked the beginning of his rapid rise in the sport.

Dwayne traveled around the world, wrestling in Europe, Asia, and the Middle East, as well as across the United States. By early 1997, at twenty-five years old, Dwayne had become the youngest wrestler to win the Intercontinental WWF title, the sport's second-highest championship.

WWF wrestlers often talk to the fans during matches. They also do lots of interviews for the WWF TV shows. Dwayne's confident personality and speaking skills shined in these moments. In the ring, his huge muscles and athletic talent also made him stand out.

His success made his next move easier. Dwayne told Dany's parents that he wanted to marry her. By finally meeting Dwayne in person, after he became a WWF star, Dany's parents gave their approval. Dwayne and Dany were married on May 3, 1997, in a ceremony that combined both their Samoan and Cuban heritages.

Later that year, Dwayne and the WWF made a big change to his character's wrestling style. Up to that point, Rocky Maivia had been a heroic character known in wrestling as a "baby face," or just a "face." A "face" is a good guy. Dwayne and the WWF decided to turn Rocky Maivia into what is known as a "heel"— a classic bad guy.

Fans soon loved booing Rocky Maivia. Dwayne ate it up, taking the microphone to trade insults with the crowd or with his opponents. As a "heel," Dwayne became more popular than ever. Then, in late 1997, he changed his name once again. While challenging champion "Stone Cold" Steve Austin to a match, he ended a speech by saying, "Your bottom line will say, 'Stone Cold: has-been!' Compliments of . . . The Rock!"

For the next two years, wrestling as The Rock, Dwayne became the biggest star in the WWF. Fans loved his famous moves like the Rock Bottom, when he slammed opponents to the mat on their backs. When he was nicknamed The People's Champion, he invented The People's Elbow. In that move, Dwayne leaped up before smashing his elbow on an opponent. He also created The People's Eyebrow, a crowd-pleasing facial expression.

During performances, he would yell out his most well-known phrases. They included, "Can you smell what The Rock is cookin'?" and "Know your role and shut your mouth!" and "Time to take you to the SmackDown Hotel!" In November 1998, The Rock won his first WWF Championship, the highest award in the sport.

When he started training to become a wrestler, Dwayne had only seven dollars in his pocket.

"The Rock," 1998

By 1998, he was making more than $400,000 a year. In 1999, Dwayne bought his parents a house. It was the first one they had ever owned in more than twenty years of marriage.

CHAPTER 4
From the Ring to the Screen

As successful as Dwayne was in the WWF, he knew he could not wrestle forever. So he looked for other ways to adapt his popularity and his skills as an entertainer. In 1999, he co-wrote a book called *The Rock Says . . .* , a best-selling autobiography. He also was offered small acting roles on TV shows, mostly just playing himself.

But on March 18, 2000, when he hosted *Saturday Night Live* (*SNL*), a live comedy show, Dwayne's flair for entertaining reached an even bigger audience than the WWF ever had. On the *SNL* stage, Dwayne's huge smile and comfortable style impressed many people who were watching. Movie producers saw how well he did and took notice. "We're always looking for emerging talent," said Mary Parent, president of production for Universal Studios. "And The Rock is definitely emerging. You can't take your eyes off him on the screen."

Dwayne approached acting just as he had football and wrestling. He wanted to learn, so he worked with acting coaches. He also met with movie producers and directors to learn how films were made. "I really wanted to be a sponge," he said later. He didn't care if it was overwhelming.

As Dwayne's film career grew, so did his family. While living near Miami in 2001, Dwayne and Dany had a daughter named Simone.

Soon, all his hard work and training paid off. Dwayne was cast as an ancient warrior named the Scorpion King in a movie called *The Mummy Returns*. Dwayne did so well in the role that a new movie was written just for his character. Dwayne set a record by earning $5.5 million for his first starring role. After *The Scorpion King* came out in 2002, Dwayne was on his way to becoming a hero in a whole new world: the movies.

In 2004, he celebrated another family milestone. On a visit to Samoa, he was given an honorary Samoan name. At a ceremony, the head of the Samoan state, Malietoa Tanumafili II, said, "From this day onward, you will carry the title Seiuli (say: say-YEW-lee), the son of Malietoa (*Alo o Malietoa*). You will leave your boyish ways behind you, as you are now a chief (*matai*) of the Sa Malietoa family, a chief of Samoa."

Seiuli was not his only name change. He also became Dwayne once again. In 2006, he asked people and the media to use his real name and not his wrestling name. "I want to be known as Dwayne Johnson the actor, and not The Rock."

With all of his success, Dwayne began earning more money. He wanted to help people in need, so he and Dany started the DJ Rock Foundation. They helped children and families struggling with serious illnesses.

In 2006, Dwayne and Dany also gave $2 million to the University of Miami in thanks for helping him get his start.

In 2008, his marriage to Dany ended. They continued to be friends and business partners, however. Dany became Dwayne's agent, which means she arranged all his movie roles and business deals. They also formed a new company to make their own movies and TV shows. They called it Seven Bucks Productions, to remember how far they had come from the day when Dwayne had only seven dollars after leaving the CFL.

The Tattoos

Tattoos are an important part of Samoan culture. The word *tattoo* is from the Polynesian word *tatau*. In 2003, Dwayne honored his Samoan roots by getting a large tattoo.

A design called *pe'a* covers Dwayne's left shoulder and part of his back and left arm. The symbols in the *pe'a* represent parts of the person's life. A large tattoo over Dwayne's heart represents his "warrior spirit." Coconut leaves stand for his role as a chief. A tortoise shell on his arm is supposed to help keep away evil spirits. Another section of the tattoo contains three parts that stand for the connection among Dwayne, Dany, and Simone. A pair of tattooed eyes called *o mata e lua* show that his ancestors are watching out for him.

Dwayne also has a large bull design tattooed on his right arm. He says that it shows "details of his personal history."

CHAPTER 5
The World's Biggest Movie Star

As Dwayne was offered more and more movie roles, he returned to the skills and discipline that had helped him excel in football and wrestling. "Dwayne started as an athlete, so he's used to being coached and pushed," said movie director Rawson Marshall Thurber. "He responds really well to that. He'll give you a hundred takes [attempts] if you want."

Dwayne is very aware of maintaining his reputation. He won't accept roles that he thinks are too "dark." That is, he won't play characters who are really awful. Tough, powerful, intense? Yes. Real bad guys? Not for Dwayne. On and off the screen, he has a reputation as one of the nicest people in the movie business, always ready with a smile and that famous raised eyebrow.

Because he is prepared to do his homework for a role, Dwayne is willing to work hard, even before shooting begins on a movie set. For his role in *San Andreas*, an action movie about an earthquake rescue, he learned to slide down a rope from a hovering helicopter. To play Hercules, he gained weight and muscle to get up to 260 pounds.

Fans have responded to his hard work in a big way. Dwayne has more than 200 million followers on Instagram, one of the world's highest totals. He posts videos of workouts, meals, fans, and family.

In 2011, Dwayne took a role as federal agent Luke Hobbs in *Fast Five,* the fifth film in the popular Fast & Furious series, one of the biggest film series of all time. Dwayne then continued his role in the sixth, seventh, and eighth films in the series.

From 2011 to 2013, Dwayne returned to wrestling for a series of matches against John Cena, a popular wrestler who had taken over from The Rock as the sport's biggest star. By this time, the

WWF had changed its name to World Wrestling Entertainment (WWE). Fans were excited to see the former champ take on the new champ. In early 2013, Dwayne, at forty years old, defeated another

champion, CM Punk, to become the WWE champion for the first time in ten years.

Movies starring Dwayne Johnson in 2013 earned more money in total than those of any other actor that year. The films included *Fast & Furious 6*, *Pain & Gain*, *Empire State*, *G.I. Joe: Retaliation*, and *Snitch*. He was the number one movie star in the country.

Then in 2015, Dwayne became a father again. He and girlfriend Lauren Hashian had a daughter, Jasmine.

Wanting to show that he was more than just an action-movie star, Dwayne returned to host *Saturday Night Live* that same year. He was very funny as President "The Rock" (similar to the Hulk) Obama in one skit, and sang a song in another.

Dwayne got another chance to sing in the 2016 animated Disney movie *Moana*. The film tells the story of an adventurous teenager named Moana who is on a quest to save her people. Dwayne's role was the voice of Maui, a demigod who guides her on her quest. Maui has many tattoos, just like Dwayne and Peter Maivia. "My

character was partly inspired by my late grandfather," Dwayne said. In the movie, he sang the song "You're Welcome." For the film, Dwayne worked with composer Lin-Manuel Miranda to become an even better singer. Today, Dwayne says that more children ask him to sing his Maui song than ask him about The Rock's wrestling career. In 2020, a short video of him singing the tune to his third daughter, Tiana, born in 2018, was seen millions of times around the world.

Despite his busy schedule, Dwayne works hard to help others. In 2016, Seven Bucks created Rock the Troops, a holiday concert for people serving in the US military. Dwayne hosted as Flo Rida and Nick Jonas, among others, performed. In 2019, Dwayne and Lauren were married in Hawaii. After the ceremony, Dwayne posted that he felt *pōmaikaʻi* (blessed).

Dwayne has also taken part in events for the Make-A-Wish Foundation, which helps grant wishes to children battling serious illnesses. In 2018, for example, he welcomed Make-A-Wish visitors to the set of his movie *Jungle Cruise*. After giving them a tour of the set, he handed out gift bags of clothing, video games, movie tickets, and *Jungle Cruise* toys.

"The kids say I inspire them, which is

awesome," said Dwayne. "But they have no idea how much they inspire me."

Dwayne's recent big movies include *Skyscraper* and *Jumanji: Welcome to the Jungle* and its sequel, in which he plays Dr. Xander "Smolder" Bravestone. His character from the Fast & Furious films starred in a spinoff movie called *Hobbs & Shaw*. In 2019, Dwayne was the highest-paid movie star in the world.

Dwayne and Seven Bucks have big plans for the future. They hope to produce *Black Adam*, a DC Comics action movie in which Dwayne will star. Dwayne is also working on a movie in which he'll play Hawaiian king Kamehameha, and has helped create a television show for NBC called *Young Rock*, based on his early life.

In 2020, his daughter Simone announced that she is going to continue the family tradition as a wrestler. Meanwhile, Dwayne continues to act and to inspire others. He has even mentioned running for president someday. According to *Newsweek* magazine, Dwayne is the third-most popular person that people in the United States would like to see run for the office! As always, Dwayne Johnson continues to be a big guy with an even bigger heart, looking to make a positive impact on the world.

Timeline of Dwayne Johnson's Life

1972	Dwayne Johnson is born on May 2 in Hayward, California
1988	Begins playing high school football in Pennsylvania
1991	Helps University of Miami win a national college football championship
1995	Graduates from Miami and joins the Canadian Football League briefly
1996	Begins pro wrestling career as Flex Kavana
1997	Wins first WWF title, the Intercontinental Championship
	Marries Dany Garcia
2001	Has first movie role in *The Mummy Returns*
	Daughter Simone born
2008	Divorces Dany, but starts production company with her called Seven Bucks
2011	Stars in *Fast Five* in the Fast & Furious movie series
2015	Daughter Jasmine born to Dwayne and girlfriend Lauren Hashian
2016	Voices key character Maui in animated Disney movie *Moana*
2018	Daughter Tiana born
2019	Marries Lauren Hashian
2020	*Forbes* magazine names Dwayne the world's highest-paid movie star for the fourth time

Timeline of the World

1976 — America celebrates its bicentennial, the two hundredth anniversary of the signing of the Declaration of Independence

1984 — The first Apple Macintosh computer is sold

1986 — In Russia, a nuclear plant at Chernobyl melts down, spreading radioactivity and damaging a huge area

1990 — The Hubble Space Telescope is launched, helping bring new views of the distant universe

1991 — The US soccer team wins the first Women's World Cup

1994 — Former longtime political prisoner Nelson Mandela is elected as the first Black president of South Africa

2005 — Hurricane Katrina causes huge damage on the Gulf Coast of the United States

2006 — Pluto is reclassified as a dwarf planet

2008 — Barack Obama is elected as the first African American president of the United States

2016 — Great Britain votes to leave the European Union, a process nicknamed "Brexit"

2020 — COVID-19 pandemic spreads around the world, killing hundreds of thousands of people and creating widespread economic problems

Bibliography

*Books for young readers

Ahmed, Tufayel. "Dwayne Johnson's Rock: Meet Dany Garcia, the Woman Behind Hollywood's Highest Earner." *Newsweek*, September 15, 2016. https://www.newsweek.com/dwayne-johnsons-rock-meet-dany-garcia-woman-behind-hollywoods-highest-earner-497885.

*Bell, Samantha S. *Dwayne Johnson*. Influential People series. Minneapolis: Capstone Books, 2019.

Fenton, Andrew. "Dwayne Johnson recalls being bullied as a kid and arrested for theft." *News.com.au*, June 30, 2016. https://www.news.com.au/entertainment/movies/new-movies/dwayne-johnson-recalls-being-bullied-as-a-kid-and-arrested-for-theft/news-story/bc2c2adc55e77670da5b30eaa612cf0e.

Johnson, Dwayne, with Joe Layden. *The Rock Says . . .* New York: HarperCollins, 2000.

*Nagelhout, Ryan. *Dwayne Johnson: The Rock's Rise to Fame*. New York: Lucent Press, 2019.

"Now It's Seiuli the Rock." *SamoaObserver.ws*. Last modified
November 9, 2018. https://www.samoaobserver.ws/category/
article/22917.

Ryzik, Melanie. "Dwayne Johnson, Star of 'San Andreas,' Is Solid.
Solid as a . . ." *New York Times*, May 20, 2015. https://www.
nytimes.com/2015/05/24/movies/dwayne-johnson-star-of-
san-andreas-is-solid-solid-as-a.html.

*Santos, Rita. *Dwayne "The Rock" Johnson: Pro Wrestler and
Actor*. Berkley Heights, NJ: Enslow Publishing, 2019.

Svetkey, Benjamin. "The Rock Is the Secret Weapon in 'The
Mummy Returns.'" *EW.com*, May 11, 2001. https://ew.com/
article/2001/05/11/rock-secret-weapon-mummy-returns/.

"The Rock's Jungle Cruise Make-A-Wish Day." September 8,
2018. YouTube video, 4:46. https://www.youtube.com/
watch?v=rVAam1kqY9g.

YOUR HEADQUARTERS ᖴᐅᖇ HISTORY

Activities, Mad Libs, and sidesplitting jokes!
Discover the Who HQ books beyond the biographies